HOW TO SURVIVE IN

The ARCTIC AND ANTARCTICA

LOUISE SPILSBURY

WAYLAND

www.waylandbooks.co.uk

First published in Great Britain in 2018 by Wayland
Copyright © Hodder & Stoughton, 2018.
All rights reserved.

Produced for Wayland by Calcium Creative Ltd
Editors: Sarah Eason and Jennifer Sanderson
UK Editor: Sarah Ridley
Designer: Simon Borrough
Cover design: Cathryn Gilbert

ISBN: 978 1 5263 0954 9
10 9 8 7 6 5 4 3 2 1

Wayland, an imprint of
Hachette Children's Group
Part of Hodder and Stoughton
Carmelite House
50 Victoria Embankment
London EC4Y 0DZ

An Hachette UK Company
www.hachette.co.uk
www.hachettechildrens.co.uk

Printed and bound in China

Photo credits: Cover: Shutterstock: Pyshnyy Maxim V, Sergey Tarasenko Jacheslavovich.
Inside: Dreamstime: Steve Allen 7r, 17cl, L“gray 16c, James Steidl 19c; Library of Congress 6c; National Science Foundation: Glenn Grant 10c, 22c, Patricia Hofmeester 13t, Chad Naughton 23c, Peter Rejeck 28cl, Derek Rogers 24cl, Mark Sabbatini 11c; Shutterstock: ALPO 18c, Andrew Buckin 14l, 26l, Pablo H Caridad 25t, Erwin F 8cl, Fivepointsix 29c, Volodymyr Goinyk 4l, 10l, 16l, 22l, 27c, 28l, Fred Hendriks 6l, 18l, Aron Ingi 8l, 20l, Karina Kononenko 12c, Nik Niklz 21t, Marteric 9t, PhotoHappiness 4tr, Armin Rose 12l, 24l, Uryadnikov Sergey 14c, Wild Arctic Pictures 4c, 20c, Jan Martin Will 15c, Gary Yim 26cr.

CONTENTS

SURVIVAL!

The Arctic and the Antarctic Circle are the world's coldest places. Here, the water is frozen into snow and ice. This makes it so dry that these places are called cold deserts.

The Arctic is a huge frozen ocean. It is covered in ice that is very thick in some places. In summer the edges of the ocean melt, but in winter it is frozen over.

Arctic

ARCTIC
WHERE: the region of the world around the **North Pole**
TEMPERATURE: can drop below -55°C in winter

I SURVIVED

In 1911 Douglas Mawson and two other scientists left their Antarctic base to do scientific research. One of the men, along with their tent, their sledge, some of the dogs that pulled the sledge and most of the supplies, fell into a hole in the ice and were lost. To stay alive, the other two men ate the dogs. Only Mawson finally made it back to base.

Antarctica is Earth's fifth largest **continent**. It is so cold that no one lives here. The scientists who stay in **research bases** in Antarctica mostly visit in the summer.

Antarctica

ANTARCTIC CIRCLE
WHERE: the region of the world around the **South Pole**, including Antarctica and the surrounding area
TEMPERATURE: can drop below -73°C in winter

KEEPING WARM

One of the biggest challenges in places with icy temperatures day and night is keeping warm. In the past **Inuit** people wore clothes made from **caribou** and other animal skins. The fur helps to trap a layer of warm air next to the skin. They also wore boots made from waterproof seal skin.

Inuit people, 1899

THE PARKA
WHAT: a hooded coat
FACT: Inuit people invented the parka, which is worn today by people visiting the poles

In Antarctica, icy winds that blow at 322 km/h can freeze your skin in seconds. Wear a hood, gloves, hat and scarf and pull drawstrings tight so that cold air cannot get in. Wear several thin, warm layers but avoid thick clothes that might make you sweat, because sweat can freeze on your body.

hat and hood

TOUGH TIP

Watch out for **frostbite**. You will notice a white patch of frozen skin on someone's face before they do. If they start mumbling and stumbling, they may be getting **hypothermia**, so you will need to get them warm, fast!

WARM CLOTHES

PROBLEM: the face and head lose heat easily and quickly
ACTION: cover head and face. Pull parka hood tight to keep out cold

7

SNOW SHELTERS

No one can survive dangerously cold temperatures for long without shelter. Scientists who come to study at the poles bring materials to make buildings because there are few trees there to supply wood. They often build bases on legs to keep floors off icy ground. It also stops snow from piling up in front of doors and trapping them!

research shelter

RESEARCH SHELTER
PROBLEM: scientists need to study in remote places
ACTION: research shelters contain everything needed to stay alive in the icy temperatures of the poles

igloo

Inuit people once built snow shelters called igloos. You can build one if you are stranded outdoors. Use a saw to cut hard snow into thick, rectangular blocks. Make a circle for a base with some blocks and then put more on top, tilting them in towards the top to form a **dome**.

TOUGH TIP

Dig an underground tunnel for an entrance and block it with a rucksack to keep in the heat and keep out the wind. Never sleep directly on the ground. Lie down on top of bags or clothes so your body does not freeze.

IGLOO
SIZE: most igloos are big enough for one family
HOW: each block of snow is about 120 cm long, 60 cm wide and 20 cm thick

FINDING FOOD

When it is very cold you need to eat more. This is because your body is using energy to try to keep you warm. It is too cold for many plants to grow at the poles, so most visitors bring their own food or catch it from the sea.

emperor penguin

EMPEROR PENGUIN

SIZE: grows up to 127 cm tall and weighs up to 45 kg

FOOD: people have had to eat penguins to survive

I SURVIVED

In 1911 Roald Amundsen became the first man to lead an **expedition** all the way to the South Pole. Like the Inuit people, Amundsen and his men ate seals and penguins. To survive, they also ate some of the dogs that pulled their sledges when they were about halfway to the South Pole.

In the Arctic, polar bears are too difficult and dangerous to hunt, so instead people catch seabirds, seals and fish. You can smash or cut holes in the ice and catch fish on a fishing line.

using nets at a large ice hole

ICE FISHING

SIZE: most ice fishing holes are about 20 cm wide

THREAT: if you smash the ice it may crack back to where you are standing

MELTING WATER

At the Arctic and Antarctic there is no freshwater. Freezing temperatures keep water frozen into stretches of white ice and snow that people cannot drink. To make drinking water, you need to melt ice and snow.

drinking melted snow and ice

DRINKING WATER

PROBLEM: Arctic and Antarctic air is very dry and it makes you thirsty

ACTION: drink at least 5.6 litres of water every day

old sea ice

Arctic ice forms from seawater. New ice is grey and hard, and is so salty you cannot drink it even if you melt it. As ice gets older, the salt drains out of it. Look out for old sea ice that is bluish and breaks easily so that you can melt and drink it.

TOUGH TIP

Do not melt snow in your mouth to get water. This can make your body even colder and increase the risk of hypothermia. The difference in temperature between your stomach and the freezing snow can also cause painful cramps.

SEA ICE
NEW SEA ICE: grey-white, thin, full of bubbles that contain salt
OLD SEA ICE: blue, thick, fewer bubbles, less salt

ANIMAL ATTACKS

Keep a look out for the polar bear, the largest and deadliest **predator** in the Arctic. Its powerful legs, sharp teeth and massive claws make it very dangerous. Its white fur **camouflages** it against the snow so it can sneak up on **prey**. It can swim fast enough to catch a seal in the water and on land it can outrun a person!

polar bear and cub

POLAR BEAR
SIZE: grows up to 2.5 m long
THREAT: powerful legs and sharp claws can kill in an instant

The leopard seal is named after the black spots on its coat. Like the leopard, this Antarctic predator is big, powerful, fast and fierce. It uses its mighty jaws and long teeth to kill smaller seals, fish and squid. Leopard seals have sometimes attacked humans.

I SURVIVED

On an Antarctic expedition in 1985, Gareth Wood was stepping over a patch of thin ice when a leopard seal burst through it, bit into his leg and tried to drag him into the icy water below. Wood's teammates managed to scare off the seal by kicking it. Wood was lucky to escape with nothing more than an injured leg.

leopard seal

LEOPARD SEAL
SIZE: grows up to 3.5 m long
THREAT: strong jaws and long teeth can injure and even kill

ENDLESS SUN

In the summer months the sun never sets at the poles. It shines all day, every day. You may feel cold but you are at risk of severe sunburn here because **ultraviolet rays**, or UV rays, reflect off snow onto skin. It is vital to cover up and wear strong sunblock on your lips, ears, chin and even under your nose.

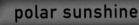

polar sunshine

STRONG SUN
WHAT: snow reflects 90 per cent of the sunlight that falls on it
THREAT: UV rays in sunlight cause redness and blisters, and can burn skin

Sunglasses are just as important here as they are on a sunny beach. Sunlight reflecting off snow can damage eyes so badly that it can cause **snow blindness**. This is when your eyes get sunburned and you cannot see well.

snow goggles

TOUGH TIP

In the past Inuit people cut slits into leather bands to make sunglasses. The narrow slits reduced the amount of sun hitting their eyes. In an emergency you can use any type of fabric to make sunglasses like those of the Inuit.

SNOW GOGGLES

PROBLEM: reflected sunlight at the poles can cause snow blindness

ACTION: snow goggles stop UV rays and protect eyes

GETTING AROUND

One of the best ways to get around on snow and ice is on a motorised sledge called a **snowmobile**. It has tracks like a tank to stop it from sinking into snow and to help it grip slippery ice. It has handlebars that turn skis at the front to steer, and help you to glide over the snow at high speed.

snowmobile

SNOWMOBILE
SPEED: up to 160 km/h
HOW IT WORKS: engine runs on fuel to power rubber tracks

In the past Inuit people made **kayaks** from **driftwood** or animal bone and covered them in seal skin. They used packs of dogs to pull their sledges. The dogs have thick coats to keep warm and wide, flat feet to grip the snow.

TOUGH TIP

Make yourself a pair of snow shoes. Bend a stick into a loop. Tie sticks across it like a tennis racket and tie it onto your foot. Snow shoes spread your weight over a wider area so you do not sink so deep into the snow.

snow shoes

SNOW SHOES
WHAT: invented by Inuit people. Made of wood with leather laces
HOW THEY WORK: wide, flat surface stops feet from sinking into the snow. Today snow shoes are usually made of plastic or metal

FINDING YOUR WAY

Everywhere looks much the same in a snowy landscape, so how do you find your way? In the past, Inuit people used the position of the sun, moon and stars in the sky to **navigate**. Watching wildlife can help, too. Most seabirds fly towards the sea during the day and return at night.

gulls

GULLS
WHAT: seabirds with a long bill and wide webbed feet. Often white with black markings on head or wings
WHERE: near the sea

Today most snowmobiles are fitted with a **Global Positioning System**, or GPS. These electronic gadgets send and receive signals from **satellites** circling high above Earth. They can be used to find where you are and to guide you to where you want to go.

I SURVIVED

On his 1914 expedition across the Antarctic, Ernest Shackleton's ship sank and the crew was stranded. Shackleton and five others went to find help in a small boat. They succeeded thanks to the navigating skills of Frank Worsley, who used a **sextant** to find their location.

GPS DEVICE

WHAT: a system that communicates with 30 satellites in the sky
HOW: links up with four or five satellites to find a location

BLIZZARD!

A blizzard is a snowstorm in which violent, freezing winds toss snow around in the air. A blizzard is dangerous because when snow whirls around, it becomes impossible to find your way across even short distances between tents, huts or vehicles. You can get lost in seconds.

blizzard

SEVERE BLIZZARD

WIND SPEED: can be anywhere between 72—160 km/h

VISIBILITY: zero

One solution is to string blizzard lines between buildings. These are ropes that people hold when they walk between buildings. If a blizzard strikes they can follow the rope to safety.

It is vital to watch the weather at all times. When a storm begins, get to a shelter quickly.

I SURVIVED

Keizo Funatsu was dog sledging across Antarctica when a blizzard hit and he became separated from his team. He dug a trench in the snow and jumped out of it every 30 minutes to do exercises to keep warm. After a terrifying night alone, his teammates found him in the morning.

blizzard lines

BLIZZARD LINES
WHAT: lengths of rope attached to posts
HOW THEY WORK: strong, thick ropes between buildings prevent you from getting lost and blowing away

CRACKS AND CREVASSES

One of the biggest dangers at the poles is something you cannot see until it is too late. **Crevasses** are deep cracks in an **ice sheet** that walkers can fall into. These cracks may be only centimetres wide at the surface, but they can be 30 m or more deep!

crevasse

CREVASSE
WHAT: ice moves slowly, all the time. This can make it split apart to form crevasses
THREAT: falling into a deep crevasse can kill a person

TOUGH TIP

Crevasses covered in snow are very hard to spot until it is too late. Most teams of people tie themselves together with a long, very strong rope. Then if one person falls the others can pull him or her back out before he or she reaches the bottom.

The problem is that these cracks are often covered by a frozen bridge of snow. If a snow bridge breaks as you walk over it, you may find yourself tumbling into the icy depths of a hidden crevasse, or even into the ocean.

SNOW BRIDGE
WHAT: build up of snow across a gap
THREAT: if you walk across one and it breaks, you may fall into a crevasse

ICEBERG!

If you are arriving at the poles by ship you need to watch out for icebergs. Icebergs are enormous pieces of ice that float in the sea. They form when chunks of ice break off suddenly from an ice sheet and crash into the water. Icebergs are as hard as rock and can make a hole in the side of any ship that runs into them.

iceberg

ICEBERG
SIZE: from 1 m high and 5 m long to 74 m high and 204 m long

THREAT: 90 per cent of an iceberg is hidden underwater

I SURVIVED

In 1912 many people believed the *Titanic* was unsinkable because of its new safety features. When it struck an iceberg that was mostly hidden underwater, it sank overnight. There were not enough **life boats** for all of the 2,224 passengers, so more than 1,500 people died.

Smaller icebergs are difficult to see before it is too late. Big icebergs are a danger, too, because the part you can see above water is only the tip of the iceberg. The part of an iceberg hidden from view below the water is much, much bigger.

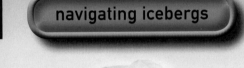

navigating icebergs

ICEBERG SAFETY

THREAT: icebergs can sink ships
ACTION: crew watches for icebergs

BE PREPARED

The Arctic and Antarctica are among the toughest places on Earth. Today more and more people travel to the North Pole and the South Pole to see these wildernesses for themselves. Visitors to the area should be prepared for anything, in case the worst happens and they find themselves stranded in the snow!

tourist boat

TOURISTS

NUMBER: more than 44,000 people visited Antarctica between 2016—2017

PROBLEM: most came in boats that would sink if they hit an iceberg

No one sets out from a base without a pack of supplies, even if they are out only on a day trip. You should always try to take food, water, spare clothes, sleeping bags, radios, cooking stoves, tents and other supplies with you. At the poles, only the tough can survive!

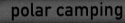

polar camping

I SURVIVED

In 2007 a ship full of tourists sank after hitting an iceberg. Its 154 passengers had only minutes to escape into life boats. Luckily a rescue ship was nearby so they had to wait for just five hours in icy temperatures, but it could have been far worse!

EMERGENCY TENT
THREAT: to survive at the poles you must stay dry and warm
ACTION: carry a lightweight, strong, windproof and waterproof tent. It should be fire resistant so you can cook inside it

29

GLOSSARY

camouflage When an animal's skin or fur matches its surroundings.

caribou A reindeer.

continent One of the seven large landmasses on Earth.

crevasse A deep, open crack in a glacier.

dome A rounded, vaulted roof.

driftwood Wood washed ashore by the sea.

expedition A trip to an area that is not well known.

frostbite When part of the body is damaged by cold.

Global Positioning System A receiving device that helps find your location on a map.

hypothermia When the body's temperature is dangerously low.

ice sheet An area of ice that covers a large area of land.

Inuit A group of people who live in northern Canada, parts of Alaska and Greenland.

kayak Boat similar to a canoe.

life boat Boat that people escape into when their ship sinks.

navigate To find one's way around.

North Pole The northernmost point on Earth.

predator An animal that hunts and eats other animals.

prey An animal that is hunted and eaten by other animals.

research base Buildings where scientists work and study.

satellite Electronic communication device in orbit around Earth.

sextant A tool for measuring angles and distances.

snow blindness Temporary blindness caused by light reflecting off snow.

snowmobile A vehicle that can move over snow and ice.

South Pole The southernmost point on Earth.

ultraviolet rays Invisible rays from the sun that burn skin.

FURTHER READING

William Grill, *Shackleton's Journey*
Flying Eye Books, 2014

Izzi Howell, *The Poles (Fact Cat)*
Wayland, 2015

Anita Ganeri, *Endurance: Shackleton's Incredible Antarctic Expedition*
Wayland, 2016

Jinny Johnson, *Polar Seas (Watery Worlds)*
Franklin Watts, 2015

Emily Bone, *Penguins (Usborne Beginners)*
Usborne, 2009

WEBSITE

Explore a wide range of objects from Antarctica in films and image banks
put together by the Scott Polar Research Institute in Cambridge, UK:
www.spri.cam.ac.uk/museum/resources/

Index